AFRICAN HISTORY FOR KIDS

Early Civilizations on the African Continent

Ancient History for Kids
6th Grade Social Studies

BABY PROFESSOR
EDUCATION KIDS

Speedy Publishing LLC

40 E. Main St. #1156

Newark, DE 19711

www.speedypublishing.com

Copyright 2018

On this book, we're going to talk about the early civilizations of Africa. So, let's get right to it!

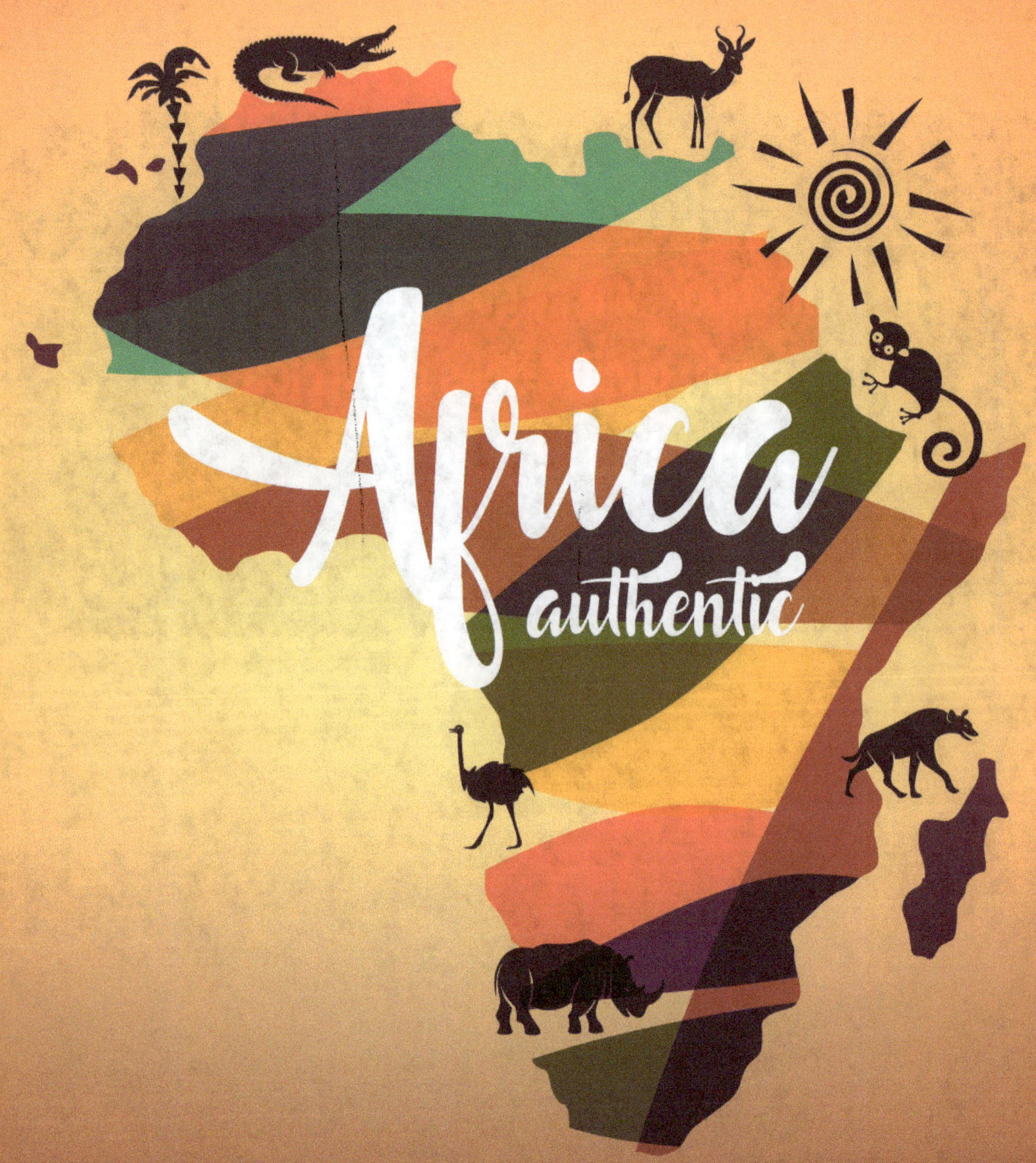

Africa
authentic

The continent of Africa had the first human civilizations on Earth. Although the most famous of these is probably the Egyptian civilization, which lasted for more than three thousand years, there were other important civilizations that also developed and became very powerful as well. They established vital routes of trade and constructed enormous cities with amazing architectural marvels, many of which are still standing thousands of years later.

ANCIENT EGYPT
(3150 BCE to 30 BCE)

The River Nile provided everything the Egyptians needed to create one of the greatest civilizations that ever existed on Earth. The river offered the needed water to grow abundant crops. The Egyptians became experts at irrigation since there were times when the water overflowed and times when it ran dry.

BABY MOSES ON THE NILE RIVER WITH HIS SISTER
WATCHING OVER HIM FROM A DISTANCE

ANCIENT EGYPTIAN STONE CARVING OF A
PRIEST CARRYING STALKS OF WHEAT

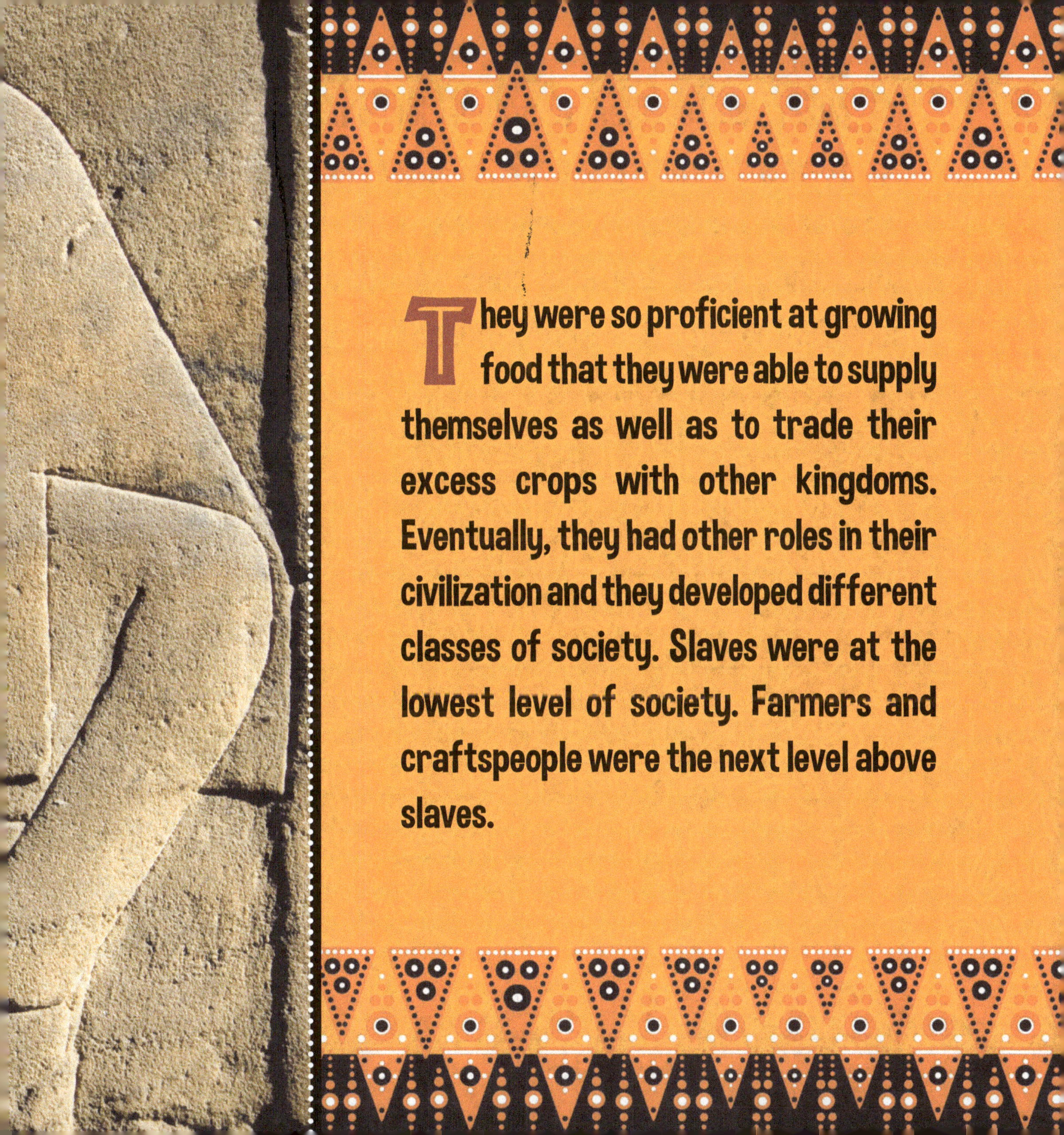

They were so proficient at growing food that they were able to supply themselves as well as to trade their excess crops with other kingdoms. Eventually, they had other roles in their civilization and they developed different classes of society. Slaves were at the lowest level of society. Farmers and craftspeople were the next level above slaves.

oldiers and scribes were considered higher class than farmers and craftspeople. Soldiers were critical to the defense of the empire. Scribes were also very important since they were the only ones who had mastered the complicated Egyptian writing called hieroglyphics.

The priests and priestesses were at a higher level than the scribes since they were important to all religious practices. The Egyptians had a complex form of religion with many gods and goddesses. They created a systematic and sacred process of mummification for dead bodies because they believed so strongly in the afterlife.

SERVANTS WAITING ON THE PHARAOH

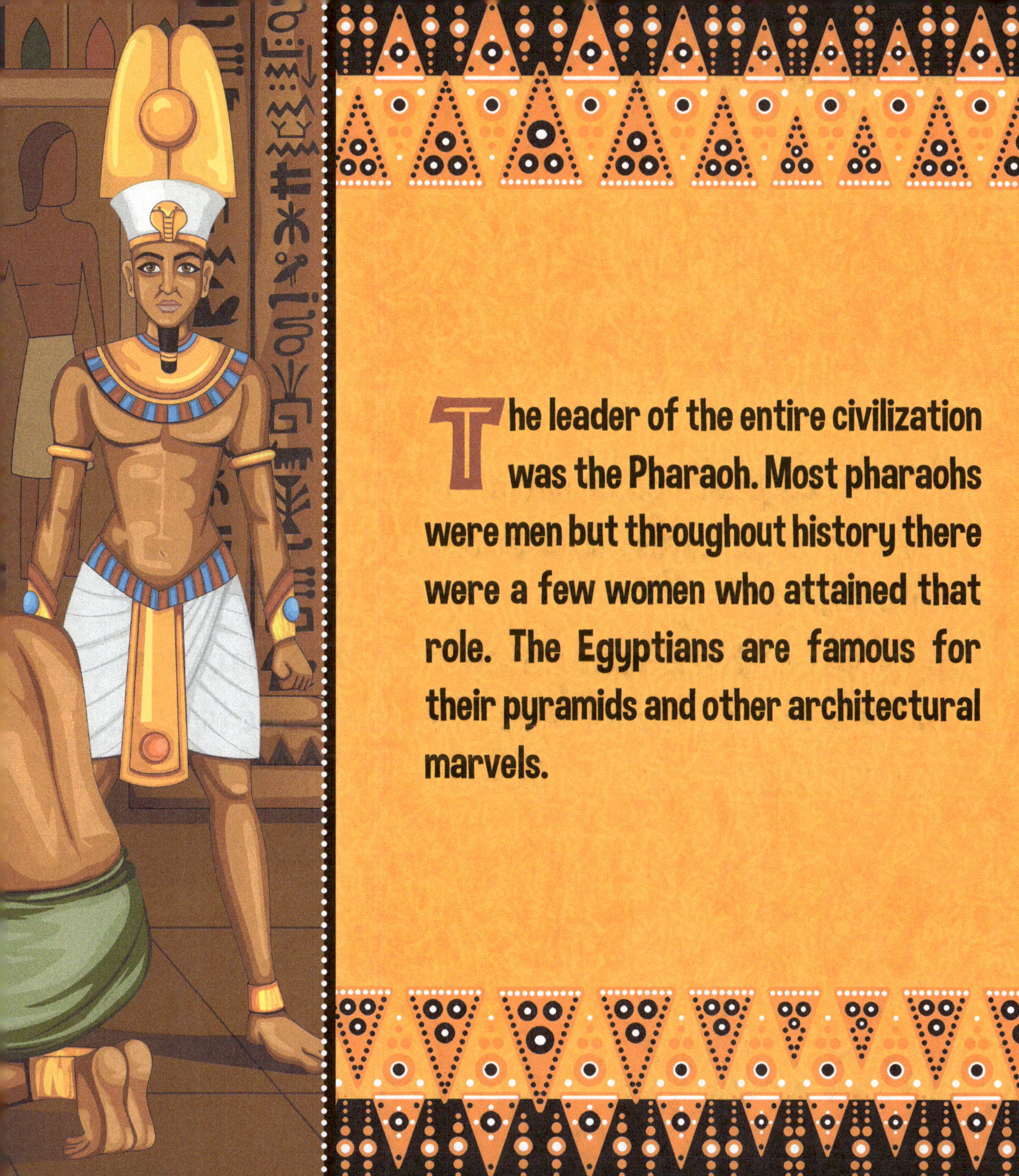

The leader of the entire civilization was the Pharaoh. Most pharaohs were men but throughout history there were a few women who attained that role. The Egyptians are famous for their pyramids and other architectural marvels.

THE MYSTERIOUS LAND OF PUNT
(2613 BCE to 1156 BCE)

The Egyptians documented the land of Punt in their writings. It was known as an exotic place that they described as "a heavenly land of gods." It was rich in precious metals and incense. They traded with the citizens of Punt for ebony, a dark wood. They also traded for gold as well as myrrh, a type of incense.

FLOTILLAS FLOTILLA ON A MISSION TO PUNT

QUEEN HATSHEPSUT

The land of Punt had many different types of animals, such as baboons and leopards. The Egyptians sent caravans and huge fleets of ships called flotillas on missions to Punt. One famous journey was the one made by Queen Hatshepsut, who was one of the few woman pharaohs. Unfortunately, the Egyptians never described exactly where Punt was located. Archaeologists are still trying to establish its precise location.

THE KINGDOM OF KUSH
(1070 BCE to 300 CE)

The Kingdom of Kush was south of Egypt. It was a powerful kingdom that survived for more than a thousand years. At its peak, this civilization controlled a huge region along the River Nile, which is modern-day Sudan. Historians know about the Kingdom of Kush and its citizens, called Nubians, primarily from Egyptian writings. It was a thriving economic hub and it gained its wealth by trading in incense, as well as ivory, iron and gold.

FEMALE NUBIANS

GROUP OF NUBIANS

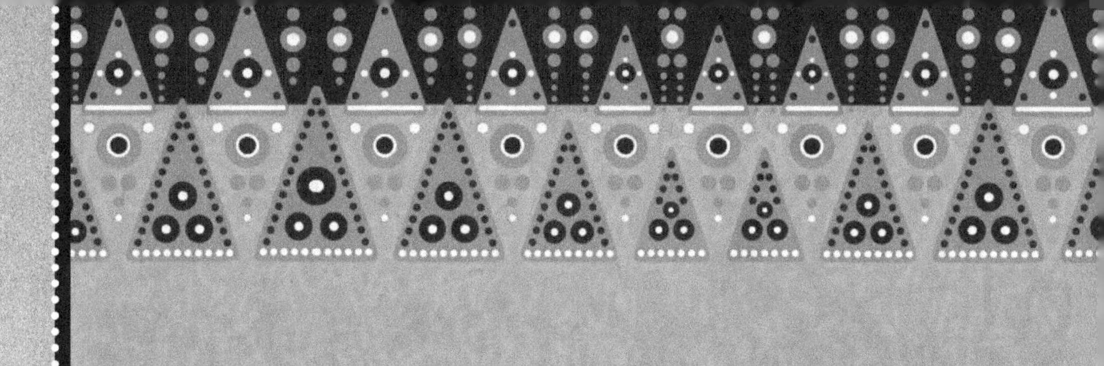

The Nubians traded with Egypt and over the centuries they were sometimes seen as Egypt's allies and sometimes seen as their enemies. The Nubians ruled the civilization of Egypt as the 25th dynasty and during that time they began to absorb some of the customs and religious practices of the Egyptians into their own.

They worshipped some of the same gods and they also performed the process of mummifying their dead.

Today, travelers to the area can still see the ancient ruins of the 200 Nubian pyramids that still stand around Meroe, which was the kingdom's capital city.

THE SMALL FISHING HARBOR IN FORMER
PUNIC PORT OF CARTHAGE, TUNISIA.

ANCIENT CARTHAGE
(814 BCE to 146 BCE)

Located in what is now Tunisia in North Africa, the city-state of Carthage began as a settlement of the Phoenicians. It grew into an enormous empire of seafaring people. The citizens of Carthage dominated trade in the area as they sold textiles and the precious metals of copper, silver and gold.

REMAINS AT CARTHAGE, TUNISIA

At the height of its civilization, almost half a million people lived there. The harbor had docks for over 200 merchant ships. Eventually, the influence of ancient Carthage extended from the

REMAINS OF THE ANCIENT ROMAN
CISTERNS AT CARTHAGE

northern part of the African continent to Spain and sections of the Mediterranean. However, this expansion began to make the Roman Empire very concerned.

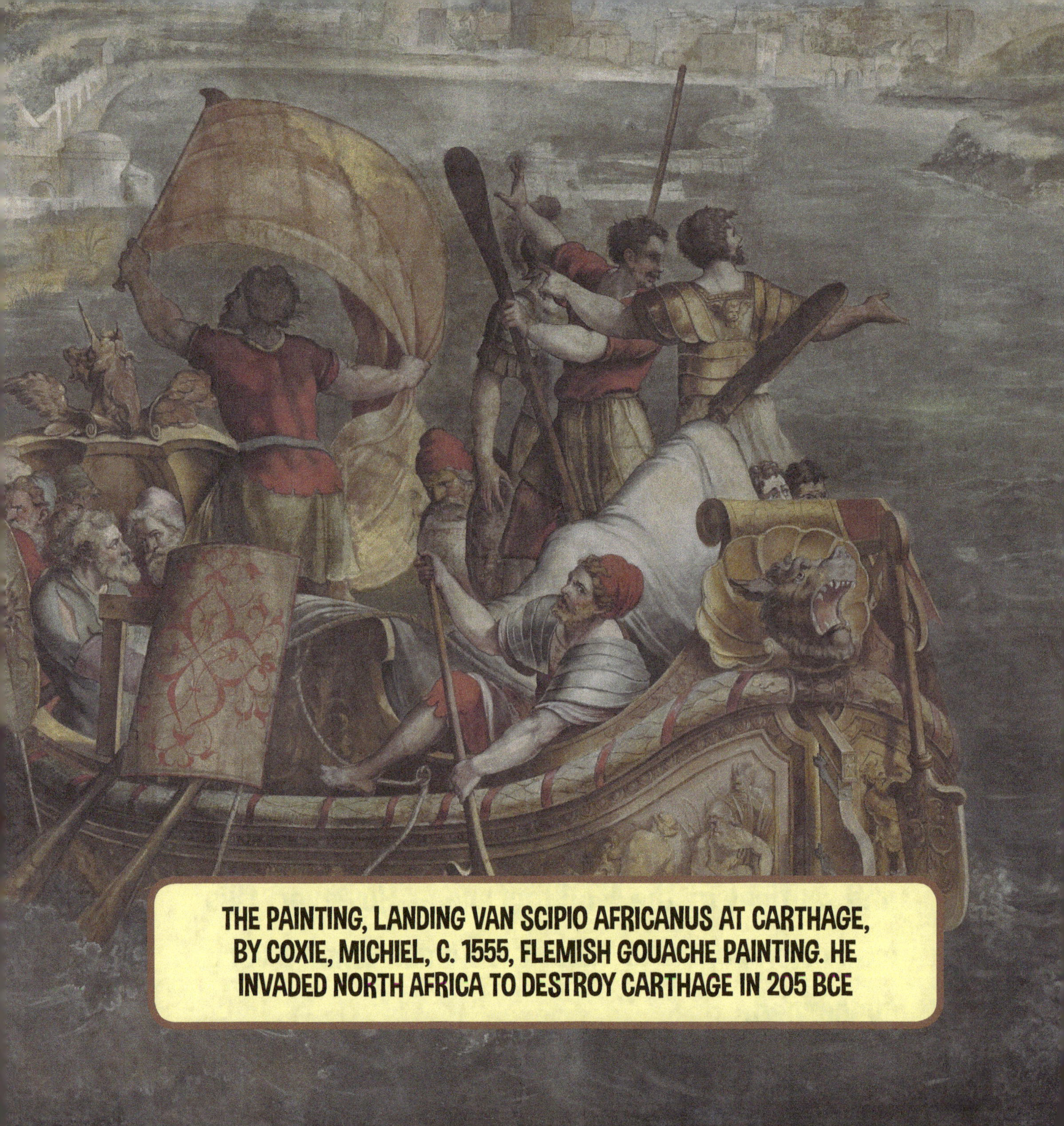

THE PAINTING, LANDING VAN SCIPIO AFRICANUS AT CARTHAGE, BY COXIE, MICHIEL, C. 1555, FLEMISH GOUACHE PAINTING. HE INVADED NORTH AFRICA TO DESTROY CARTHAGE IN 205 BCE

The Romans were not about to give up their dominance in the Mediterranean away easily. Beginning in 264 BCE, the Romans and the Carthaginians battled in the violent Punic Wars. There were three wars and the Romans were victorious and destroyed Carthage. Only a few ruins remain today.

THE KINGDOM OF AKSUM
(400 BCE to 940 CE)

During the era of the rise and fall of the empire of Rome, the empire of Aksum was in power in the lands that are today's countries of Eritrea and Ethiopia. Historians have little information about the start of Aksum, but by 100 CE it was a vital trading hub in the area.

THE STELE OF AKSUM IN ETHIOPIA

THE STELE OF AKSUM IN ETHIOPIA

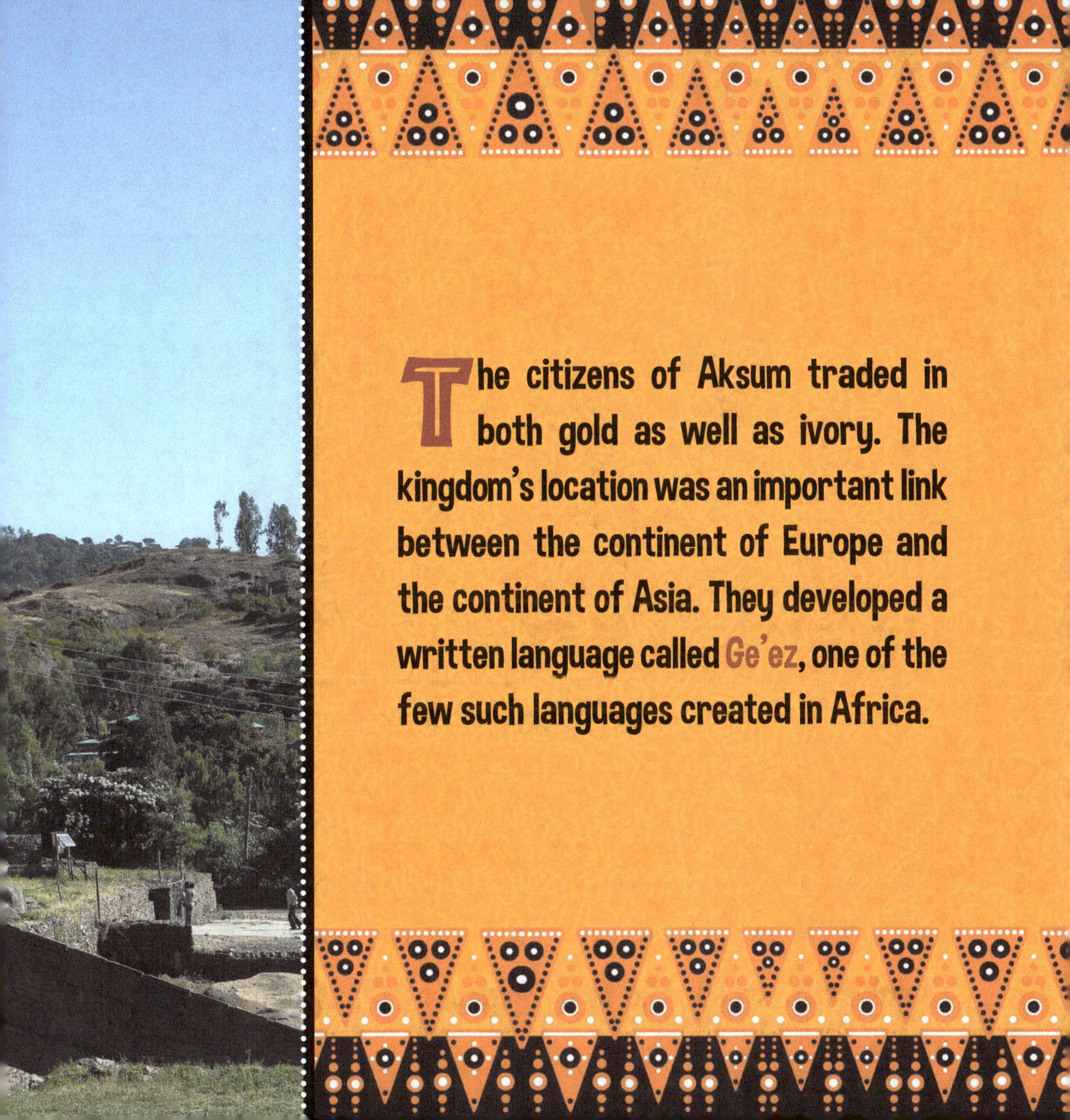

The citizens of Aksum traded in both gold as well as ivory. The kingdom's location was an important link between the continent of Europe and the continent of Asia. They developed a written language called Ge'ez, one of the few such languages created in Africa.

On addition, they developed a unique style of architecture. They constructed enormous obelisks made of stone, which were 100 feet in height or taller. Aksum was one of the first empires to accept the new religion of Christianity and these

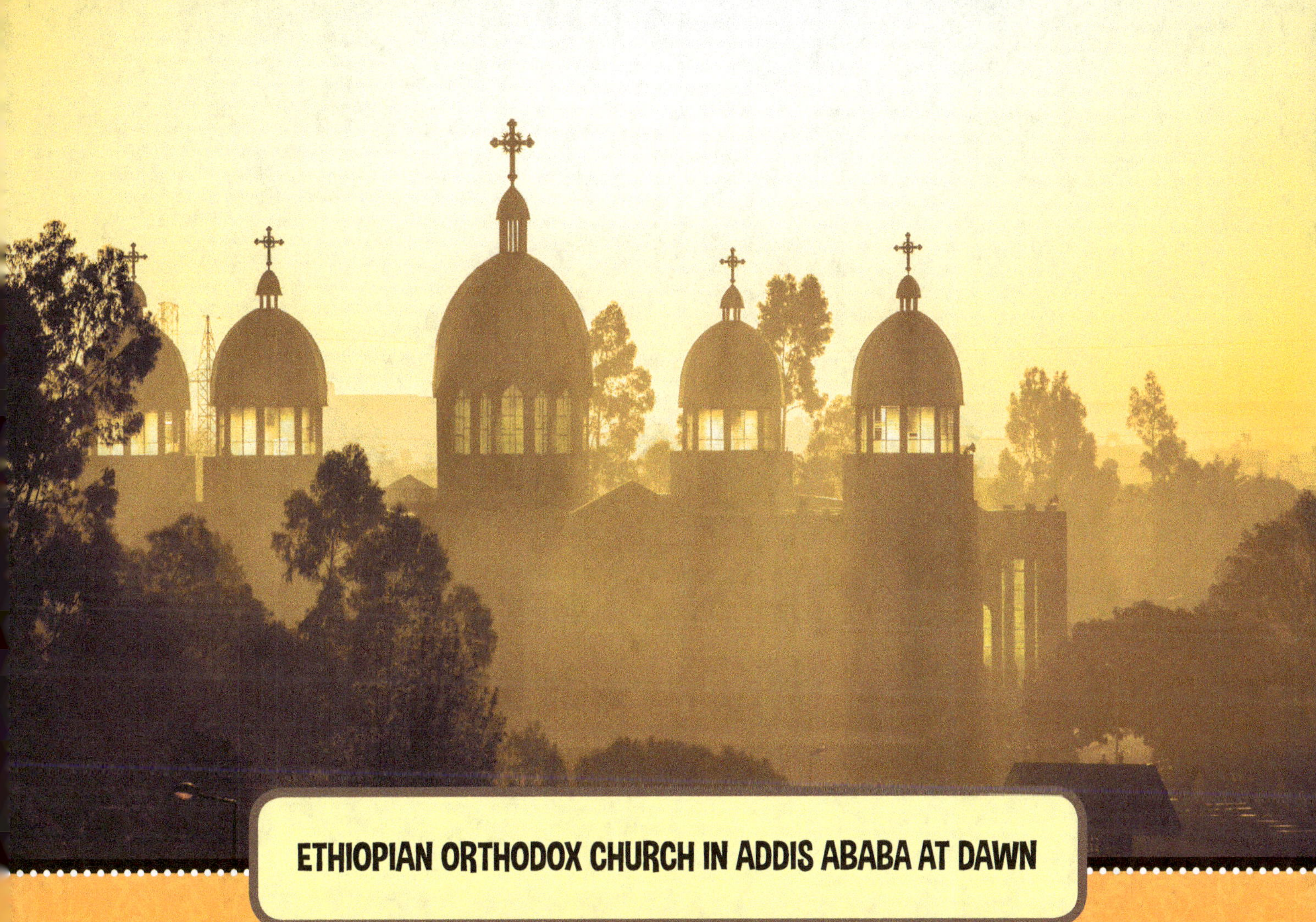

new beliefs led them to develop an alliance with the Byzantine Empire. The Orthodox Church of Ethiopia carries on these Christian religious traditions today.

CASTLE IN ACCRA GHANA

THE KINGDOM OF GHANA
(300 CE to 1100 CE)

The Kingdom of Ghana was established in the western section of Africa. Their wealth derived from the mining of two important metals-iron, which was used for tools and military weapons, and gold, which they used primarily for trading for the livestock and cloth they needed.

They organized camel-driven caravans to transport their exports and imports across the wide expanses of desert. Although they actively traded with many Muslims, they had their own religion. When the leaders of Ghana refused to convert to the religion of Islam, they were under constant attack until their empire weakened and collapsed.

THE GREAT ZIMBABWE RUINS NEAR MASVINGO
IN ZIMBABWE, SOUTHERN AFRICA

THE GREAT ZIMBABWE
(1200 CE to 1400 CE)

In the sub-Saharan region of Africa there is a huge stack of stone towers and fortress walls that were cut and assembled from enormous pieces of granite. This is the location of the Great Zimbabwe, the capital city of a huge, native empire. Today, the region that made up this large empire is composed of the country of Botswana, as well as the country of Mozambique and the country of Zimbabwe. This empire was along a trade route that connected the region's gold mines with the Indian Ocean's coast and seaports.

Very little is known about this mysterious stone capital city, but artifacts that archaeologists have found there, such as pottery from China, glass from Arabia, and fabrics from Europe, point to the fact that it was a thriving

hub of trade and commerce. It's estimated that over 20,000 people lived in the capital city during its peak. It was abandoned in the 15th century and no one knows exactly why.

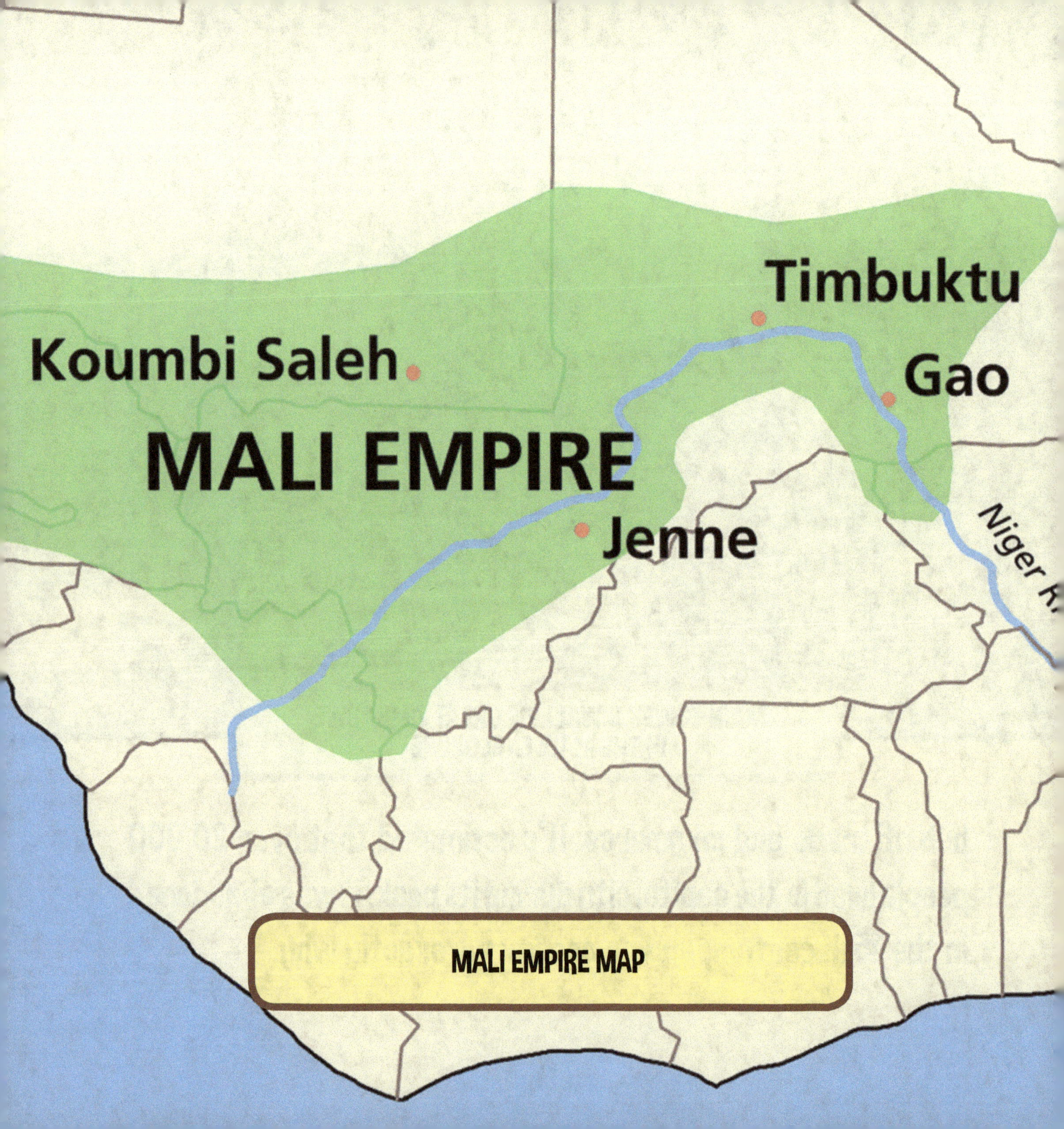

Koumbi Saleh
Timbuktu
Gao
MALI EMPIRE
Jenne
Niger R.
MALI EMPIRE MAP

THE MALI EMPIRE
(1235 CE to 1600 CE)

In the 1200s, a powerful leader by the name of Sundiata Keita led an uprising against a Sosso ruler. He united and organized the citizens into a new kingdom. Under the rule of Keita and subsequent leaders, the Mali Empire gained control over a large region of western Africa.

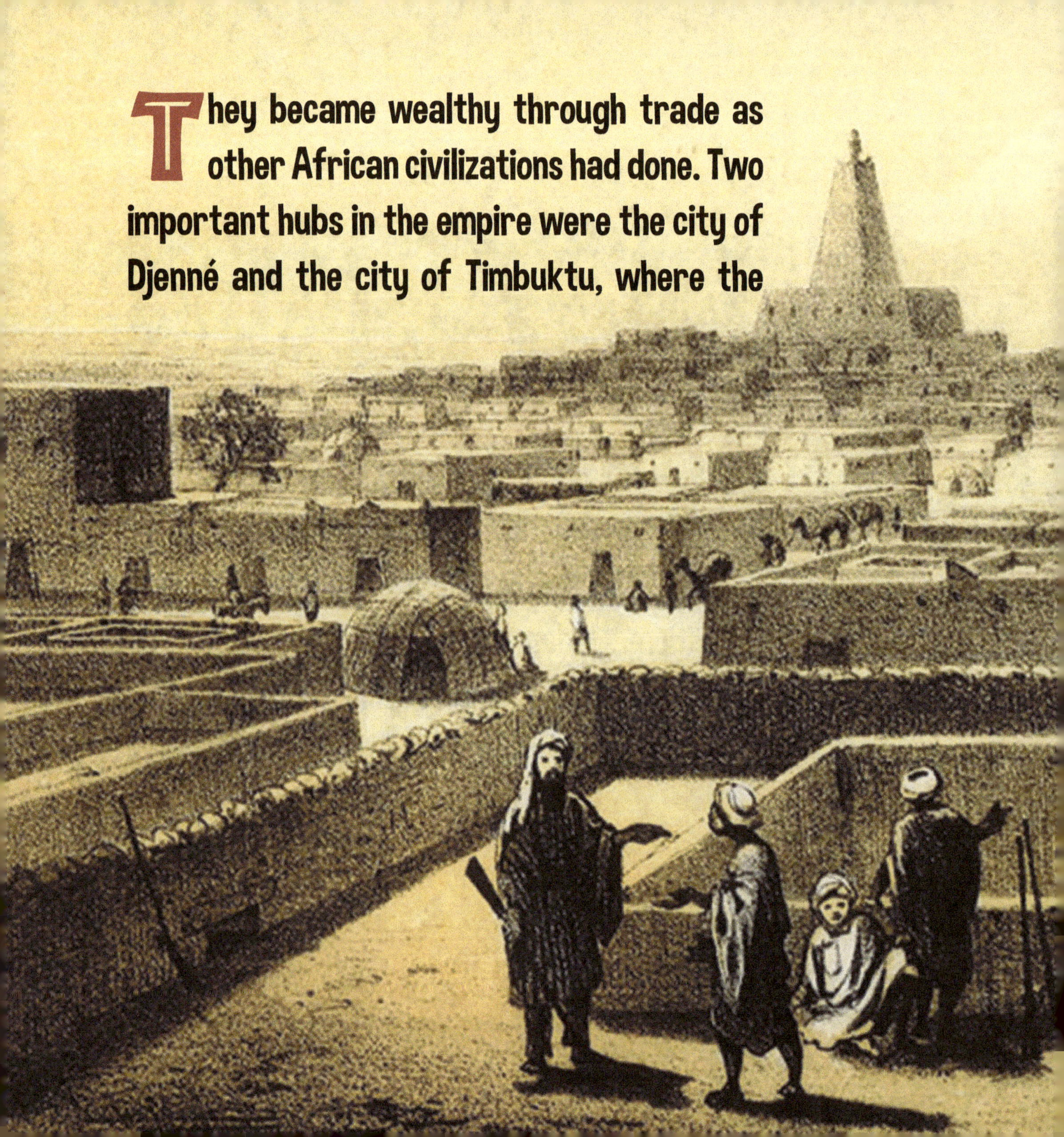

They became wealthy through trade as other African civilizations had done. Two important hubs in the empire were the city of Djenné and the city of Timbuktu, where the

Muslim culture flourished with beautiful mosques and schools dedicated to the study of Islam. In Timbuktu, the library at Sankore University was known for its huge collection of over 700,000 ancient manuscripts.

tagaza
aqueſt ſenyor
mulſe melly ſe
de gincua/aq
rich/el pus n
eſta ʒ rida el
qual ſeazull
bu
SINIA
ʒougeu
MANSA MUSA

At its peak, the empire was known for its immense wealth. In the 14th century, one of its famous rulers named Mansa Musa stopped in Egypt on his way to make a sacred pilgrimage to the holy city of Mecca. He was accompanied by a huge entourage and he gave away so much gold along the way that the decrease in demand caused the precious metal to become devalued in Egypt for years afterwards.

SONGHAI EMPIRE
(1464 CE to 1591 CE)

The Songhai Empire was established from some of the former regions of the Mali Empire. As the Songhai Empire grew, it expanded to a size greater than all of Western Europe. Today, the region where the empire was located is composed of a dozen countries. The wealth of the empire was established through trading with other kingdoms.

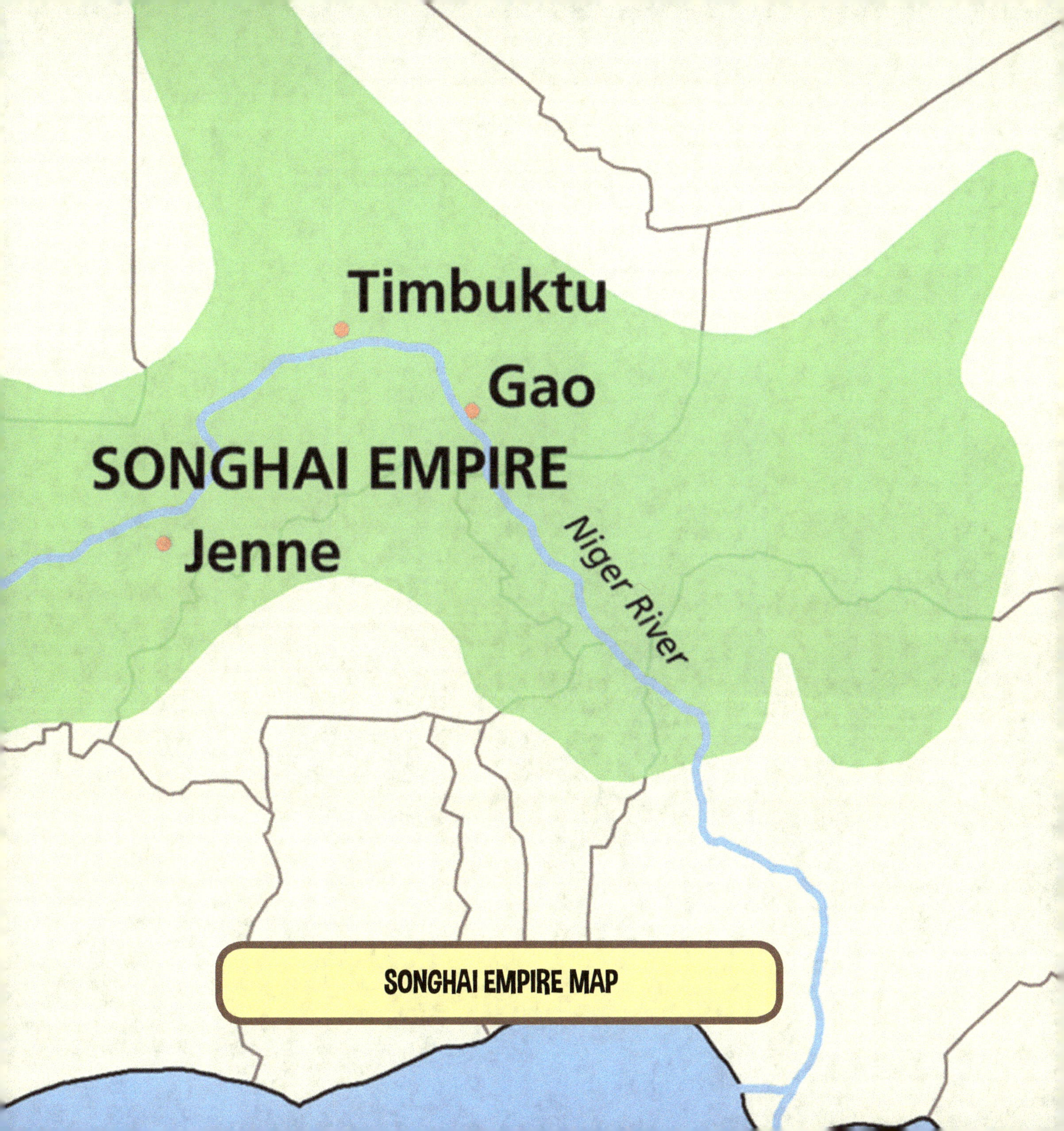

Timbuktu
Gao
SONGHAI EMPIRE
Jenne
Niger River
SONGHAI EMPIRE MAP

THE CITY OF TIMBUKTU

This empire had a sophisticated government. Its land was organized into various provinces and each had a governor. Its golden age occurred under the leadership of King Muhammad I Askia. He expanded the empire by conquering new lands and created a strong alliance with the Caliph in Egypt.

He began hundreds of schools for the study of Islam in the city of Timbuktu. It was a very powerful empire until in the late 1500s there was a civil war that made it vulnerable. The Sultan of Morocco saw the opportunity to invade the empire when it was at this low point.

SANKORE MOSQUE IN TIMBUKTU

ANCIENT OBELISKS IN AKSUM, ETHIOPIA

SUMMARY

The Egyptian civilization wasn't the only great civilization that was established on the African continent. Like their Egyptian neighbors to the north, the citizens of the kingdom of Kush built great pyramids in their lands along the Nile River. Many of these pyramids can still be seen today. The people of the kingdom of Aksum constructed very tall stone obelisks that were marvels of engineering.

Many of the kingdoms throughout Africa became very wealthy due to their trade in precious metals and other rare items, such as incense, ivory and ebony.

At one time, the Sankore Library of the Mali Empire contained over 700,000 manuscripts. For thousands of years, different kingdoms throughout the continent of Africa reached new heights of civilization.

Now that you've read about the early civilizations of Africa, you may want to read about the geography of Africa in the Baby Professor book, A Quick Introduction to the African Continent - Geography Books for Kids Age 9-12 | Children's Geography & Cultures Books.

Visit

BABY PROFESSOR
EDUCATION KIDS

www.BabyProfessorBooks.com

to download Free Baby Professor eBooks
and view our catalog of new and exciting
Children's Books